Up the Tall Tree

Acknowledgments

Executive Editor: Diane Sharpe
Supervising Editor: Stephanie Muller
Design Manager: Sharon Golden
Page Design: Simon Balley Design Associates
Photography: Heather Angel: page 7 (top right); Bruce Coleman:
cover (all), pages 6-7, 7 (bottom right), 9, 12, 15, 19, 21, 23, 25;
Oxford Scientific Films: page 11; NHPA: pages 13, 17.

Library of Congress Cataloging-in-Publication Data

Hankin, Rosie.
    Up the tall tree/Rosie Hankin; illustrated by Kareen Taylerson.
        p.   cm. — (Read all about it)
    Includes index.
    ISBN 0-8114-5738-9 Hardcover
    ISBN 0-8114-3748-5 Softcover
    1. Oak — Juvenile literature.   2. Oak — Ecology — Juvenile literature.   [1. Oak.   2. Forest ecology.
3. Ecology.   4. Trees.]   I. Taylerson, Kareen, ill.   II. Title.   III. Series: Read all about it (Austin, Tex.)
QK495.F14H345   1995
583'.976—dc20

94-28179
CIP
AC

1 2 3 4 5 6 7 8 9 00 PO 00 99 98 97 96 95 94

Up the Tall Tree

Rosie Hankin

Illustrated by
Kareen Taylerson

STECK-VAUGHN
COMPANY
ELEMENTARY · SECONDARY · ADULT · LIBRARY

4

This oak tree is very old. It has
taken hundreds of years to grow.
Look at its huge trunk.

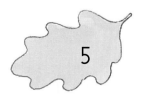

The oak tree has hundreds of roots that run underground. They hold the tree firmly in the ground. The roots get water from the soil.

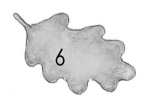

Look at the fallen leaves!

Animals such as slugs, worms, and spiders
live in the fallen leaves.

The bark protects the tree.

I can see little insects running around on it.

Many insects and plants live on the bark. They even get their food there. Do you see the stag beetles?

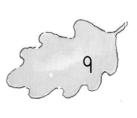

The oak tree has seeds that are called acorns.

They look like eggs in little cups.

Acorns fall to the ground in the autumn. Every oak tree starts as a seedling that grows from a tiny acorn.

11

They are not acorns. They're called galls. In the spring, the gall wasp lays its eggs on the tree. Then the bark swells around the egg and makes a gall.

12

The egg grows inside the gall and then hatches. When the wasp has grown, it makes a hole in the gall and flies away.

That is a thrush's nest. These birds use
mud, grass, and twigs to build their nests.

In the spring, the mother thrush lays her
eggs in the nest.

A squirrel uses twigs and leaves
to make its nest.

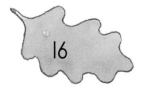

16

Squirrels collect acorns and nuts to save for winter food.

There are some bats hanging upside-down.

Shhh, don't wake them up.

Bats hide in leaves and sleep during the day.

18

After the sun sets, bats wake up and fly around looking for insects to eat. They have special ears that help them find their prey in the dark.

19

This kind of oak tree has leaves that change color and fall to the ground in the autumn. By the time winter comes, it will have no leaves.

These leaves are different. They're green and shiny.

Those are ivy leaves. The ivy plant grows in the ground near the oak. It climbs up around the tree trunk. Ivy is evergreen and does not lose its leaves in the winter.

The mistletoe's roots grow into the branches and trunk of the oak tree. It steals its food and water from the tree.

22

The mistletoe has sticky white berries
that birds like to eat. Mistletoe
berries are poisonous to people.

That bird is called a nuthatch. It has pushed the nut into a crack in the bark. Now it will break into the nut and eat it.

The nuthatch eats insects, too. It runs
up and down the bark, looking for
things to eat.

When it starts to get dark, the owl comes out to hunt for food.

26

The owl flies very quietly, looking for mice and other animals to eat.

I'm getting hungry, too. Let's go home for dinner!

Can you name the animals and plants on this page? The answers are on the last page, but don't look until you have tried naming everything.

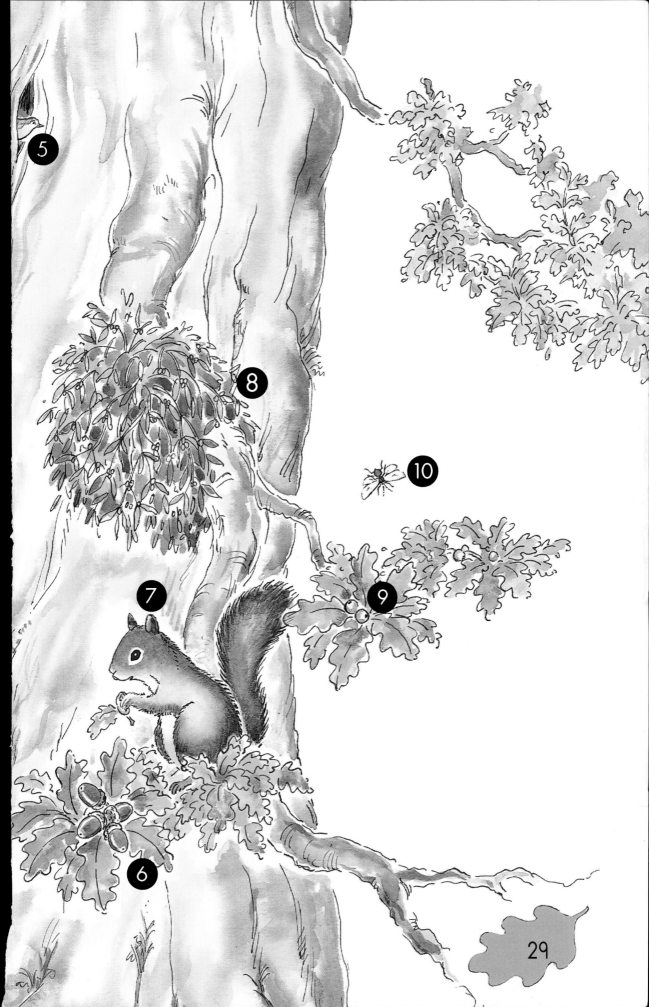

The animals and plants in this book are shown at different sizes than they really are. This is how they look compared to you.

Stag beetles

Ivy

Acorns

Spider

Mistletoe

Gall wasp

Galls

Owl

Bat

Squirrel

Nuthatch

Thrush

Oak seedling

Index

31

Answers: 1. Thrushes 2. Nest 3. Bats 4. Ivy 5. Nuthatch 6. Acorns
7. Squirrel 8. Mistletoe 9. Galls 10. Gall wasp